AuthorHouse™
1663 Liberty Drive
Bloomington, IN 47403
www.authorhouse.com
Phone: 833-262-8899

This book is printed on acid-free paper.

ISBN: 978-1-6655-0878-0 (sc)
ISBN: 978-1-6655-0880-3 (hc)
ISBN: 978-1-6655-0879-7 (e)

Library of Congress Control Number: 2020923462

Print information available on the last page.

Published by AuthorHouse 03/31/2021

authorHOUSE®

This book was edited by ***Mauzoun***,
a creative writing studio based in Jeddah, Saudi Arabia.

Illustrations by Nada Purlo

MAUZOUN
CREATIVE WRITING

4

A Dedication to My Keepers
To my beloved parents, who support
me unwaveringly.

To my four siblings, who never fail to
bring me joy.

To Abeer Fada'ak, my rock during school years.
To Dr. Alaa Habib, my light in medical school.
To Arideth Pison, my dear Alaskan friend.

6

Passion for Memories
A Collection of Poetry
by Dania Mohammed Jamjoom

Table *of* Contents

Beginnings

An Introduction by Dania

Here, you are invited to ride a rollercoaster of memories with me, which has two opposing poles: the lowest of lows, those of sadness, gloom, and grief, and the highest of highs, representing utmost joy, happiness, and the willingness to simply let go and have fun. In Passion for Memories, you will not only read my poems: you will read my innermost thoughts and my remarkable journeys, both beautiful and disheveled.

The process of sharing my poetry has been transparent, vulnerable, and raw. Here, I speak to the world from the very depths of my heart, hoping that my words reach the very depths of your heart, too.

What you have in this book is my heart, bare and tender, enclosed in your hands. Please take care of it, and most importantly, let go, be free, and enjoy the ride-- life is too short, and there's way too much fun.

Passions

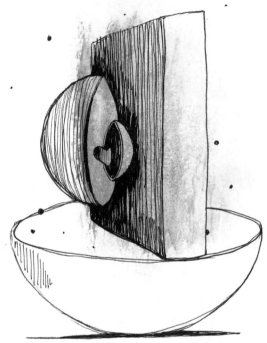

Differences

Some are big. Others, small.
Some are short, and the rest, tall.
Some are slim, others are fat,
round like a ball.

But friendships and relationships
shouldn't depend on any of those at all.

It depends on having a great personality
that makes people want to fall and sink
into the warmths of your heart.

To crawl and seek the sunshine of your smile.

But personalities these days are
unimportant no more.
It's the looks that people fall for.

So, it doesn't matter if you're nice or sincere.
It all depends on the looks: the bad boy talks
that girls love to hear, or showing off
when boys are near.

But I don't care about what they want,
what they like, or what they say.
I will never change,
not tomorrow,
not today.

I Love You

I will always be the light that shines on their paths.
I will always show them the way they should
have walked from the very first day.

I love you like I've never loved anyone else before.
I love you like a bee that thrives on a rose.
I love you like rain that ceases to exist without clouds.
I love you like a mama bear that can't part from her cubs.
I love you like a dark sky that's always seen the moon.
I love you like a new day that's always known sunshine.

I'll tell you what I think when I walk past a garden,
and pass by a beautiful rose, so pink, so small.
Its scent is so fragrant: I will think of you
before I have time to blink.

A Birthday Wish

The sun shines in the sky,
The birds are chirping in the trees so high,
and the soft smell of spring passes by,
all wishing happy birthday,
from me, Dania, to you.

Wednesday, April 11, 2001

Look Around

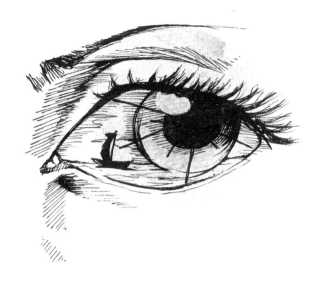

You sometimes look at people and say,
"Oh, they have friends in every way,"
who make them happy throughout the day.

We look around, and there we see:
something shining, so brightly.
We look deeper, and there we find:
someone special, oh so kind.

Someone who brightens up your day,
and straightens you up in every way.

And finally, we realize and see,
that we're oh so lucky,
because we have thee.

Thursday, February 15, 2001

Birthday Wishes to Duaa

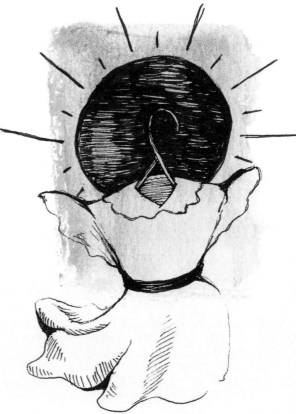

You woke up one day, wearing
your dress blue and grey.
You brushed your hair,
you put on some spray,
then tied your shoes and went to say,
"Hey, you! Today is my birthday."
But I shouted at you right away.

I didn't want you to know that we may
have planned out a birthday for you today.

Later that day, we went to the beach to play,
figuring out how to give you something that may
bring you happiness, on this special day.

So here we are today to say,
"Happy birthday!"
I hope you have a beautiful day.

Wednesday, January 3, 2001

Mom, you are like a star shining so bright
in the cruel darkness of the night.

You are the glowing rose that comes and goes,
in the hands of those whose love they chose.

You are the air I breathe into my lungs, and
the kind words spoken off my tongue.

You are the bird chirping very early in the morning,
the sweet smell of early spring, the delightful
taste of dark Swiss chocolate.

I thank you for bringing me into this life,
for holding me so tightly, and caring
for me day and night. You are an angel
from heaven, the best friend ever given.

Tuesday, March 20, 2001

For You, My Dimo

The days have past but are yet to come
I always knew you are my number one.
I know that sometimes I always do–
things that are not so good to you.
I scream so loudly, and make you cry.
I know that's why I feel like I'm a fly–
a fly that should always be squashed
with a book, a foot, or a brush.

I think of what happened there that day.
I could have stopped it. I know I could.
But, I lost control, like a lousy troll.
But that doesn't mean I love you, no.

You are the one––I know you are
the one who makes me fly above the sky,
to a world filled with happiness and joy,
and come back like a little boy.

I beg you to forget what I do,
because sometimes, I'm grouchy,
that's true. But in the end,
we both know we love each other,
and that will grow.

Friday, December 1, 2000

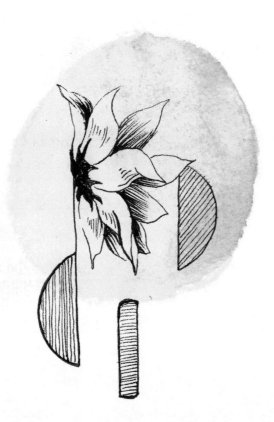

To Sarah

Be nice to me,

        don't be mean.
'Cause I like you––
        do you know what I mean?!

Try to be keen,
because surely,
that's the way to be clean.

Wednesday, December 6, 2000

Remembrance

I remember the day
when we used to play in May
and swim in the cold waters of the bay.
I liked it then, wouldn't you say?
I thought we'd be together until this day.
But you left me alone, you ran away.
I won't let you do that again.
Oh no, no way!

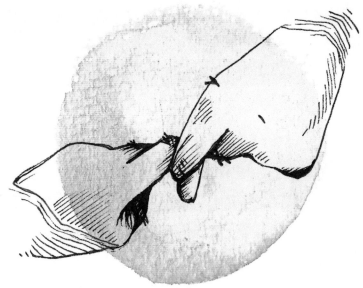

Auntie

Hi, auntie. How are you.
I miss you. How about you?
How is the weather?
It's cold, isn't it true?
I hope you're not ill,
or down with the flu.

But most of all, I want you
to pray to God to forgive me and you
for the bad deeds we sometimes do.
I hope He forgives us, don't you?

How is everybody?
I hope they're not blue.
Say hi to Uncle Ahmad,
Grandpa and Aunt Azza too.

Tuesday, December 19, 2000

To You, My Doodi

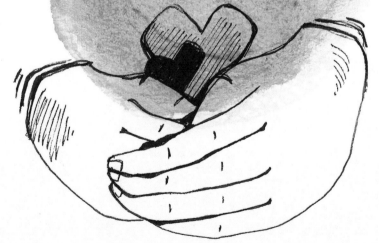

I am your sister and your friend.
I write for you words so true.
You are my sister, and I love you.
You are the friend that helps me through
the worst of days, when I am blue.

You sometimes get on my nerves,
and make me do things which
are not so good to you.
I can't stop it. It's hard to do.
Please try and tell me what you'll do,
and I'll try to always be gentle to you.

That doesn't matter, by the way.
Just listen to the words I wish to say,
these words of wisdom and honor that may
give you a smile, and lighten up your day.

Be good to your parents, and try
not to be stubborn, like an old hat!
Don't listen to people who tell you
terrible things, and make you blue.
Don't do unto them the same things
they've done unto you.
Just do the things
that make God love you.

You have your sisters,
and if you lose your friends,
you won't need any more,
because we're here for you
until the furthest end.

Wednesday, December 20, 2000

Going Away

The days come and go,
but you will still show
that you are a good friend to them,
and we will all agree.

When we grow up and leave school,
I hope that we will still be friends, if that's cool.

You have a smile that brightens up the day
and brings happiness in every way.

January 22, 2001

A Time to

Grow

The sun and moon have left the galaxy,
the birds and butterflies have left the skies,
the seas and oceans have lost their waves,
because they've all seen the precious gift
of human race.

Friday, June 7, 2002

To My Cousin

The sky without stars,
like sleep without dreams
like music without a song,
like a rose without scent,
like a face without a smile
like me without you.

My Sister and Me,

Part I

Best friends are we
my sister, and me.
They say we look alike,
but we're different, aren't we?

Hey, you!
No matter what I say,
no matter what I do,
I will always be there for you
--that is true.

No matter what time
brings us towards,
I want you to know that
I loved you, always,
and I still know I will.

Nothing will part us.
Believe me, I know.

I say the truth,
I know i do.
So believe me or not,
you will have a clue.
I assure you.

Wednesday, December 6, 2000

My Sister and Me,

Part II

Today is the day that you go away.
I guess we have to say goodbye
in a sad and gloomy way.

I can't believe it,
I can't, no way.

Hey, people, did you hear
that she was going away?
Imagine the minute that you fly away.
What will happen to our world, today?

The sun will turn from orange to gray.
The moon shall quickly fade away,
and the birds sitting on trees will fly away,
all wishing to be close to you until the day
you come back and make the sun say, "Hooray."

Tuesday, May 1, 2001

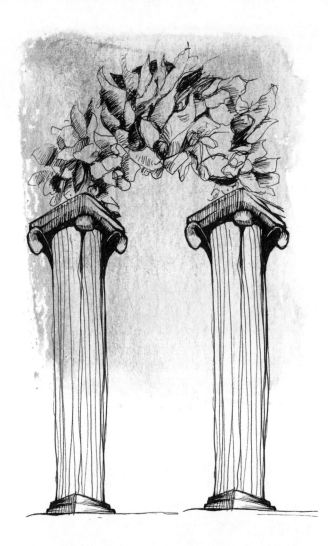

To My Pillars

You're the best parents in the world, Mom and Dad.
You gave us strength and courage.
You showed us the cliff between good and bad.

You took care of us when we were little.
When we become old, or become bald,
I'm sure you will still take care of us, too.

You made us warm from the thunder and storm.
You made us feel safe in our comfy little home.
You made us feel safe from the insects that bite.
You taught us to say: thank you, please,
good morning, and good night.

Of course, you did not forget
to teach us Allah's rights: to pray, to thank,
to worship throughout the night.
I thank you from the bottom of my heart,
because without you,
I wouldn't have grown this strong.

Memories

Upside-Down

I woke up one day with a cough and a flu.
I looked at the skies, and gosh, they're so blue.

I wonder why I always think of you.

You've filled my life with things so new.
it was too late when I realized it was true.

I really have a bad crush on you.

Who Are You?

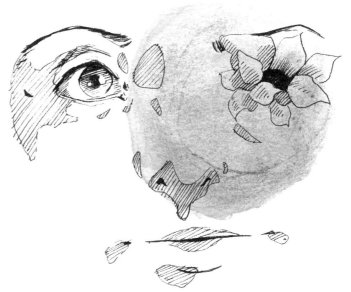

Who Are You?

You know me in a way,
and I think I know you, too.
I tried to guess who you are,
and I think I approximately knew
because all roads lead to you.
Could you tell me, so I could
be sure that it's true?

Tuesday, January 23, 2001

Featherless

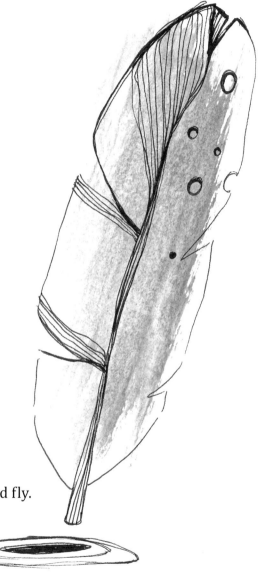

The sun sets in the sky,
the birds fly so high.
I always push myself hard to try
to spread my wings like a bird and fly.
But instead, I sit there
without giving it a try.

Tuesday, August 7, 2001

A Moment of Grief

What shall I do? This is so bad.
Why do all of you try to make me sad?
It was so difficult, until I knew
how to make myself glad,
how to live a life I've never had.

But you messed everything up,
you messed it up so, so bad.

Why does everything have to turn
out worse than the first one had?

I think I'm going to become so sick and so cold.
I'll look like sixty when I'm only nineteen years old,
or be the fleeting snowflakes that children love to hold.

I wish I could think of nothing sad,
but my mind has nothing to do,
and thinks of all things that are bad.

I always thought I could change the world,
and tell everyone that evil has been sold:
sold to the devil, and changed to something
as pure as gold. But you can't change anything
these days. That is what I was always told

Swept Off the Shore

The days go by without you by my side.
I've been swept off the shore by a big, strong tide.
I tried to get closer to you, I swear I tried,
but failed because I always lied.

I lied about my love, my passion,
my feelings for you inside.
I thought that all of it will end fast
like a rollercoaster ride.

But I'm so stupid.
I can't get you off my mind.

Wonders of Life

I sit here and look at the wonders of life:
how God created them all in a perfect way,
that not one color could ever be put on display.

I look at everything big and small,
I look at the tiny things that crawl.

They, too, have reasons on this Earth they call.
Or, if it weren't so, then God wouldn't have created them at all.

Set your eyes around you.
There is no reason to stall.

Tuesday, August 7, 2001

Dark Path

I walk alone on this dark path,
a dark path that no one has set foot on.
I continue to walk, furiously letting
everything I have ever felt fall through.

My fear, my anger, and what you
made me feel throughout the day.

It's creepy out here, with loneliness and a scare but I found out that I truly don't care.

The trees, so tall, surround me.
I suddenly fall into this hole
and fall, as I go faster and faster
and faster, then stop.

I have hit the ground
with barely a sound.

Friday, September 7, 2001

Tough Luck

Today is the day I go to where you do not stay.
You hurt me badly, you made me sad.
I love you so much––you know I do.
I hope you love me, too.
You deceived me, you made me fall for you.
You are so selfish.
I wish I had a clue.

But I didn't––too bad for you.
I will forget you now.
I don't want any more of you.
This the end: love me, or
not, you have to choose.

Tough luck to you.

Thursday, October 1, 2009

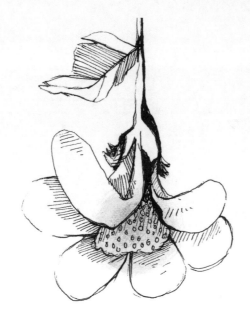

Forget

Me

Today is the day I go away.
I'm leaving and staying far away.
You hurt me badly, you're making me run
away. I hate you, and I don't want you to stay.

Don't come looking for me anymore.

Saturday, October 3, 2009

A Leap
of Faith

Last year, I was in jail.
I was locked and left alone.
It's freaky, and will give you a scare.

I had problems taking care of myself.
I lost my writing and walking skills.

I really wanted to die.

I felt that God was punishing me for
something And that made me cry. But then, I
realized,
that it was a test of love and purity.

I learned a lot. I toughened up.
I became stronger. I have lost
control of myself, but I shall
go on, and this is why
I will forever be strong.

Friday, October 23, 2009

Love me, Too

We went to the beach with family and
friends. We had fun that never ends.
We swam, tanned, and played games.
I hope that this will never change.

I love you, I know I do.
I hope that you get a clue.
But more so, I hope that
you love me, too.

Friday, November 6, 2009

The End

Maybe I will die
before I say goodbye.
I could get run over by a car,
or get stabbed by a knife
and pass through a journey so far.

You won't be happy,
and your flame will die,
because you will have no one else to blame,
except for a picture kept in a rusty frame.

Your claims are so small, and I can't see.
Is her mother's love like air to tree?
I always think of myself as doing things right,
studying hard in the depths of the night.

But if I did the slightest mistake,
suddenly I'm evil, and can't live with light.
I guess it's me who is lost, after all,
in the darkness of the night.

Printed in the United States
by Baker & Taylor Publisher Services